T0196789

MY LIFE *and* SPIRITUAL GROWTH *as a* MILITARY SPOUSE

MARTHA E. H. FRANKLIN

WESTBOW
PRESS®
A DIVISION OF THOMAS NELSON
& ZONDERVAN

WestBow Press books may be ordered through booksellers or by contacting:

WestBow Press
A Division of Thomas Nelson & Zondervan
1663 Liberty Drive
Bloomington, IN 47403
www.westbowpress.com
1 (866) 928-1240

First Edition

Designed by Martha H. Franklin
Edited by The Liddell Group
Library of Congress Cataloging-in-Publication Data
Franklin, Martha H.

ISBN: 978-1-5127-6250-1 (sc)
ISBN: 978-1-5127-6249-5 (e)

Library of Congress Control Number: 2016918071

Print information available on the last page.

WestBow Press rev. date: 08/04/2017

DEDICATION

This book is dedicated to my parents, Creola and
Wiley Hickenbotham, and grandparents

To my angels – Benita Stallworth, Mary Liddell,
Barbara Walton, and Annie Hayes. I love you
and thank you for your love on this journey.

Special recognition to my nieces and nephews
who I love. You are all close to my heart.

Kyle Jason Franklin, thank you for all the life
experiences, I have learned through growth.

I love you guys with all my heart!

CONTENTS

PREFACE

I am a native of Pensacola, Florida. I spent many days at Pensacola Beach with my family enjoying the salt life! Therefore, I am truly a beach girl who has been riding the waves of life ever since.

Shortly after leaving home, I became a Marine military spouse while working as a government DOD employee.

In this book, I share the benefit of my personal development and gained wisdom, even during my darkest days... I'm certain, as I stand in the light, I'm blessed and a gift from God. No one knows where their journey ultimately ends, but I do know it begins with us. I have a lot to share and I believe that you will come out on top no matter what life throws your direction.

Standing in the light; know it is a blessing and gift from a higher power!

My God.

ACKNOWLEDGMENTS

Special recognition to all military service members and their spouses. Thank you for your support in defending our nation.

INTRODUCTION

I'm Martha Elizabeth Franklin-Hickenbotham. I was born in Pensacola, Florida.

And I have been in your shoes, as a new military spouse. Maybe you're trying to figure out how to make all the ends meet and need to get a job on base. Or, are you away from home and your closest friends for the first time and pulled from your faith?

I was there, too.

Married more than twenty years to a 1st Sgt in the Marine Corps, I came into my gifts and the fruit of the spirit when I fell on some hard and dark times of my life.

That's when I really saw my gift from God – how I healed myself from stress heartbreaks, by faith and the Holy Spirit. There were days that I would awaken and darkness will speak death over my life. There were days when I would have sickness attacks on my mind, turning people against me who were dear to my heart. There were also days when I experience, shutting down of my finances from employment. I experience six years of dark times in my marriage falling apart. When I tried calling people, no one responded, but I fell on my knees crying for dear life.

I asked God for strength. My Transformation began.

I am now a spiritual leader starting a ministry with 200 spouses and civilians.

I am healthy, happy, and full of grace. Please never give up. Stand tall in your dark times in life.

I knew I wanted to give back to my military spouse family-that is when WOMEN OF FRUIT AND LABOR 53# came alive.

I started to prepare a snapshot of my life in 2000. It was not a good picture. I look at my snapshot in 2017, and it is working for my good. I have hit the golden snapshots of my life by God's grace. I pray you all will get on board and allow my staff and I to start preparing for you a snapshot of your life.

···

Chapter 1

WINTER DAYS AND NIGHTS MARTHA PCS ORDERS AND RELOCATION

K yle and I dated for six months. We met in Washington on January 7, 1995, and married June 19th of the same year. I was happy, excited, and as goofy as I could be. We lived comfortably at our first duty station at Headquarters—the U.S. Marine Corps, Washington D.C. base. Financial stability felt so good! At 29 years old, I must say we were doing quite well. Our bills were paid with a considerable amount of money left over for rainy days. We purchased a new Honda Accord, a Suzuki motorcycle and lived in an upscale apartment- The Gables in Rockville, Maryland. We enjoyed each other and all life had to offer.

My spouse and I found out we would receive a set of permanent changes of station (PCS) orders to New Orleans. I was so excited to move to New Orleans because it is only two hours and 59 minutes away from my hometown of Pensacola, Florida. When I submitted my two-week notice — I worked at a Montessori preschool in Germantown, Maryland — the thought of leaving my coworkers made me very sad because I loved my job.

We set up an appointment with the S-4 (Logistics/Embark Office) for a pack-out of our household goods. However, the orders to New Orleans fell through, and we were not going to be able to execute our PCS move. I was speechless. At the time, my husband was only a corporal, and my job had already been filled at the Montessori Preschool. The bills still had to be paid, so I applied for new jobs. The first jobs I applied for were off base in the metropolitan area of Rockville, Maryland. I applied at the local shopping mall and nearby department stores. I knew I would not make the previous rate of eleven dollars an hour, and babysitting for some parents from my previous job was a big pay cut for me. I was not comfortable with the pay I received. Department stores would pay about seven dollars per hour, but I needed a job, so I took one at Montgomery Ward.

Two months later, a paycheck of 400 dollars every two weeks was a joke. Some of our bills were late; car loans fell behind. Credit scores fell. The stress level increased between my spouse and me. I thought, *Life sure is something. One day you are up; the next day you are down. How do you prepare for that?* Well, you can't. I felt drained. Waking up every day was like the movie *Groundhog Day.* I was dark inside.

I casually walked through Montgomery Ward and said to myself, "Martha, stay focused!" Then one day I had an eye-opening experience when I spoke with my coworker April who had nothing. She never had money for lunch. I took her home one night. Her living arrangements opened my eyes wide. I realized just how blessed I was. There were some families who had it more difficult than we did. I was very thankful to be on someone's payroll.

A couple of months after this realization, Kyle spoke to another Marine, William. He explained that I formerly worked for the government in Pensacola, Florida, at the Naval Air Station in 1990 as child care teacher for pre-toddlers. The Marine gave my husband some advice for me how I could get back in Department of Defense Civilian job system. The human resource office (HRO) information William passed along helped me. I decided to apply for a child-care provider position at Anacostia-Bolling Air Force Base. This seemed like a good idea and an excellent opportunity. I went to the HRO on base and applied for a general schedule (GS) position. I received a callback for an interview. It went well, and I was offered a Monday through Friday position with morale welfare recreation (MWR) working with pretoddlers in 1996. But my heart and mind were still set on a GS job because of the government benefits.

I was employed in Anacostia-Bolling Air Force Base MWR for seven months. I was happy to be on the payroll and enjoyed my job working as a child caregiver. I loved the kids and enjoyed their energy. Even without kids of my own, I felt as though God appointed me as a caregiver. I can only imagine what it must be like to have children, especially if you are a single parent. I believe children need loving caregivers in their lives.

I know there were many military spouses with greater responsibilities than mine. I observed these spouses when they dropped off their children. I felt it must be so hard for them, but they stuck with it. I also noticed there were many military spouses, struggling. I could see the stress on their faces. We all must be strong, or we risk the possibility of breaking. Therefore, I felt it was my duty to help relieve that stress and give those spouses my joy and smile to assure them their children were in good hands. The spouses grew to trust me, and I forged strong bonds with my fellow caregivers. My job was to give my joy to the kids. I loved them like they were my own children. It appears the children were with my fellow caregivers and me more than their own parents. So, I kept in mind that spouses must look out for each other.

I traveled an hour each day to and from work. However, it was worth it. I was so happy when the housing office called to tell us we were next in line to move on base. By this time, I was a GS employee. I worked hard and advanced quickly, giving God the glory for everything.

It was exciting to move to Anacostia-Bolling Air Force Base. It was only five minutes away from the child care center, so I could go home for lunch. Base housing sits in the middle of Washington D.C. and is in a completely different location from the military base.

We still received phone calls from bill collectors. This made us focus on working to get out of the financial nightmare. Every penny we made was accounted for. It took three years to pay off all our bills. We made so many sacrifices.

I watched my base kids grow. In my classes, I taught numbers, colors, animal, sounds and songs; that included, of course, "Wheels on the Bus." Those were just a few of the activities we did.

I worked well with the children's parents. Many parents requested their kids be placed in my class. This made me smile with joy because it meant they felt secure leaving their children in my hands. It must be a good feeling to know your kids are in good care.

My coworker Linda and I were there for each other at work. Each of us were responsible for five kids. Some days I would take a child who was having difficult time out of her group, and she would do the same for me. We loved the kids very much. We also bonded well outside work. We talked about personal things in our lives.

Kyle and I were doing well by then. My husband had been accepted to drill instructor (DI) school in San Diego, California, for thirteen weeks. Even before going to DI school, he was always away from home. Communicating was hard. He would call, and sometimes I would miss his call. I did not like that at all. The thirteen weeks are so intense, you are grateful when you can hear his or her voice.

You know the drill. I remained behind in Washington D.C., at Anacostia-Bolling Air Force Base, where we were stationed. What a never-ending story. I felt like I was living life on my own. This was when I stepped up my game and took care of myself. I married a Marine, so that made me a Marine as well.

We may not be on active duty, but the job of a military spouse never ends.

My hat goes off to spouses who hold down the household and take care of their children until their spouses' return. We do not have children, so it was just me, but the thirteen weeks my spouse was away were long and daunting. I paid all the bills, which was a good thing. But there were fewer phone calls. When he returned from school, our amount of debt was in a good place. Then, a new set of PCS orders came through. I was so sad to leave my class. This time we were moving to San Diego, California.

I knew we received travel pay, and I prayed we would be okay until I found another job. This was what had become of our life together, so I had to stay open and positive always, even though trials. Do not create any extra debt. Without extra debt, the move won't be so hard on your family's finances. Create a budget that works for the entire household. Our bills were completely paid off before leaving for San Diego.

I was so sad to leave my kids and coworkers, but I had no idea my season would be up so soon. Time flew by so fast. I never knew where the road would take me, but I knew it was good because God and I maintained spiritual conversations. This was when my faith started to be tested- traveling a road I knew nothing about, and not seeing but believing.

There is a government program designed to help spouses who travel on orders but a lot of military service members and their spouses are not aware of it. I could get on the Priority Placement Program (PPP). If you travel on orders with your military member and are a GS employee, you are eligible to be placed on the PPP list. This allows you to have a job at your spouse's next assignment. But, you must follow up with the HRO Office in your area. During that time, I worked for the school district in San Diego.

One day, I received a phone call from Ms. Lewis who worked in HRO within the metropolitan area of San Diego. Even though we didn't know each other, she advised me to move into the medical field, because childcare did not have a lot of growth. I never worked in that field before, so I wondered, *Wow! Will I succeed in the medical field?* Then a realization hit me. This was a higher power at work. Once again, he blessed me with his grace. I was humbled. So, she transferred me out of the caregiver field and signed me up as a medical clerk. That landed me a job at Balboa Naval Medical Center.

....

I was sixteen when I got my first job as a caregiver at Greater Mount Lily Baptist Church, the church I attended. Since then, all I had ever was a caregiver of children. Even though being a caregiver was what I knew best, change is always good. As I started to feel myself grow, it was time to branch out and try something new.

The move and the new job caused high levels of anxiety and fear. However, after training for two weeks, I was placed in the labor and delivery department, helping deliver babies. I loved my job. I had the pleasure of seeing firsthand the gift of human life that a higher power created here on earth. I do not have children of my own, yet where he put me I was a medical clerk.

Whether it's a deployment, training, unaccompanied tours, and so on, our loved ones who serve are always away from home. Sometimes you get lonely and want attention. On the other hand, I was blessed and grateful to be able to embrace great people around me. You must be strong by bringing faith into your life. I worked from 3:00 p.m. to 11:00 p.m. at the Naval Medical Center Labor and Delivery Department. It was not bad job, and I enjoyed what I did. It's my calling. I truly believe this idea in my heart, you have put yourself in the company of good people. Also, believe He will put them in your life. I, myself, live by these words.

"I believe I can do all things through Christ who strengthens me."

My spouse worked at his unit from sunup to sundown. He was never at home; what a never-ending story that was. He was the "new hat" on the block of his new unit, so he really did not know how it operated. It was a crazy experience I do not wish on anyone.

After working on the labor deck in San Diego for two years, I received the call of my life. My husband and I were at home in San Diego. I was watching TV and he was in the shower. My mother-in-law, Kristal, called and asked to speak with Kyle. My mother-in-law sounded different. I couldn't explain the energy to you. I took him the phone as he dried off. Then, all at once his face changed, and a strange feeling came over me. I knew something was wrong. Kyle wrapped the towel around him and walked with me to the living room.

He sat me on his lap and said, "Martha, something has happened to your mother." She had passed away. I felt weak and sad. My sister Ann could not call me because she was too upset, so she called my mother-in-law. My mother had suffered years of serious nerve conditions that affected her mentally and physically. I wept like a baby in my husband's arms.

I am the baby in my family. I always thought I had to be strong. Even though I felt dark and empty inside, and with everything going on in my life, I remained strong and prayed through it. I missed my mom so much. She was a great praying woman who raised five girls on her own.

Unfortunately, my father, Wiley, drifted in and out our lives. He was never consistently there for us while we were growing up. My mother, Creola Hickenbotham, suffered from depression and a broken heart. On May 5, 2000, my mother went to be with my God, after negligence in a nursing home. My father, Wiley Hickenbotham, was killed. I will not go through the story of how he died. For me this is a lot but I decided to live. I cry somedays and I will never forget this, but I let go and let God.

We had funeral services for my mother in Pensacola, Florida, at the church I grew up attending. I cried the entire time, but still thought I needed to be strong. I needed to be a powerful military spouse. I had drilled it in my head. I'll later explain how holding things in can make matters worse. You must cry and let it out. I have come to realize we are spiritual beings having a human moment.

Finally, our three-year tour was up on the drill field in San Diego in December 2001. We received orders to Japan for a one-year unaccompanied or two-years accompanied tour. We decided I would move to Germantown, Maryland, for the year. I thought it was a good move for me to go back to where I had family.

In coming days, I called the packers to see when I would receive our household goods. I was told the following day. The packers showed up around 1:00 p.m. the next day. I was so upset because the mover was by himself and an older man who could not lift furniture. Luckily, my sister made a few phone calls to find some strong men to help move my household goods inside my new home.

As the guys started to bring things in, I realized a lot of my items were missing. This triggered a red flag. Some of our household goods made it, but we were missing a lot of personal items, including a bed frame, and bathroom items for the master bathroom. Things from Pier 1 Imports were also missing. I called Logistics to report some of our household goods stolen and had to file a claim for the missing items.

I arrived in Maryland in December of 2001. It was cold and I stayed with my family for a week before moving into my apartment. Everyone sat around, enjoyed the snow as it fell ever so slowly outside while my sister Barbara cooked dinner, including her great stuffing. My sister is a great cook, so dinner was delicious. It was great to be around my loved ones. I had received the key to my apartment at The Kinston, but we were without household goods, and my husband had not arrived from San Diego yet. Unfortunately, we had to wait for the movers to deliver our shipment. This is common for spouses and family members.

The next morning, I awakened and took a shower. The weather changing caused me to feel a little under the weather. I went to breakfast at my sister Barbara's house. I prayed the movers would come with my household goods. At that point I was back to Square One, getting the house together and looking for employment in a new city.

I said to myself, "I can do all things in Christ Jesus! He is the one who strengthens me!"

I went to Barbara's later and had a girls' night out at her house.

Boy, did I need that relaxation. It was still snowing outside, and music played inside. It was such a pretty, white Christmas. It was so good to talk on the telephone with family members in other states. My sister's girlfriends are good, positive

At the same time, I was dealing with my mom's recent passing and my husband's leaving in thirty days to be stationed in another country. I had only a box spring and no frame for the bed. I slept on the floor of a nice apartment. We still did not feel Okinawa would be good for me. Fear set in, mostly because I feared leaving the county. I believe every military spouse can stand in my shoes on this matter. I'm not sure why I allowed the thought of moving to Okinawa to cause fear in me. I did not realize at the time that this was anxiety. I was the tough girl on the outside, but deep inside I hid in fear.

My husband drove back to Germantown, Maryland, after I had lived in the apartment for about three weeks. I was delighted to see him, since we would be able to spend New Year's together. We had an amazing New Year's!

I slept well our first night in the apartment, even though we didn't have all our household goods. The next morning, I found a couple of pots, some silverware, and plates in a box. I cooked dinner, which included the traditional black-eyed peas for New Year's. And yes, there was a dime inside of it for good luck.

At the time, I attempted to draw unemployment, routinely calling once a week to check on my status. Once again, we lived off one income.

When Kyle flew out to Japan, I was so sad. He had a safe flight, but I missed my husband dearly. We made sure to talk at least four days a week. Being away from each other was difficult. This type of marriage can take you spirit apart, if you allow it. I prayed the travel pay would hit and his paycheck would be on time. I remained on edge about money. This was a test I knew I would get through, and I did.

One day shortly after Kyle went to Japan, after I woke from a nap, I chose not to unpack anything. I got dressed and went to my sister's house. We went out to dinner. Once we returned, we sat around and talked. I still did not unpack anything but, rather, called a girlfriend in Los Angeles. Her words of encouragement were good to hear. She said "Martha, you are strong woman. You can do this." Sometimes you need to hear such words from friends. Reading my Daily Word was extremely helpful and everyone gave me a lots of positives feedback. I would get back in the GS system.

In the meantime, my husband served our country in Japan. I missed him. The weather started to get bad, and I wished he was with me.

I spoke with family over the telephone for a little while it snowed. It was so cold outside, but so pretty. And my husband called. You know the drill. He needed to tell me that his pay was messed up. I took a deep breath and stayed calm, because it was just good to hear from him. Everything would work out, because even during a crazy day I couldn't let everyone know.

I called the company that packed us out of San Diego about my missing household items. I was told a check would be cut for me when I filed a claim for the missing items. To file the claim, I had to go to the base with my general power of attorney (POA). The claim was in, and I waited for a check in the mail and slept on the box spring. I had to keep my faith that something would be worked out. I felt like I was stuck in the *Twilight Zone* or the movie *Groundhog Day*. Life can be crazy sometimes.

I took it easy and tried to relax. I watched a movie on television. I prayed my husband's check would be in the bank a lot sooner than later. Fortunately, talking to all my girls helped to keep my spirits up.

"Hang in there, diva, you can do this," they prayed over the phone with me.

I did not sleep well, because my mind constantly raced. I hated to worry about how we would pay bills. Plus, my unemployment had not hit yet. I also believed that if I worried, my higher power would feel I did not trust Him. His will is to do great things in my life. Suddenly, my husband called and said his check would be posted Friday. All I could say was "Thank you!" In addition, the unemployment office called a few hours later and told me that I was approved to receive 500 dollars a week. Defense Finance and Accounting services would send the check for the missing household goods in the mail the next week. In life, we must realize that sometimes we cannot fight our battles alone. Therefore, we need to give it all to the higher power. My God supplies all my needs. Whatever higher power you believe in, put it out there in the universe.

Shortly after, on a Friday afternoon, my girlfriend called me and said she was coming over to hang out with me. I picked her up from the train station, and we went to eat dinner at my sister's house. Afterward, we went out on the town and had a nice time. I was so happy to see her. We hung out late at night, so we decided to sleep in until ten o'clock. We got up, showered, and got ready for the day. We kept the party going some more by going out to dinner followed by dancing and cocktails that night. Once again, we had so much fun. Every spouse needs this type of activity sometimes.

I started to get back in the gym because exercising makes me feel good. It helps me to sleep well at night, it keeps my spirit up, and I love the way it makes my curves look! I work hard on my body and keeping in shape. A healthy body always leads to and assists in developing a healthy mind and spirit. When the body is healthy, military spouses can concentrate more efficiently on completing our daily tasks even in times of stress and anxiety.

Some of my family called to check on me while my husband was stationed overseas and some didn't. Unfortunately, some family members are in their own worlds. You know how it is. Family will be family.

In the meantime, I called the Civilian Human Resources Office (CHRO) in Maryland. My focus at this point was to gain employment in the GS system. I began to feel that staying behind was the wrong decision. We spent money for the apartment, and we could live in base housing together in Okinawa. Spouses should always travel with their loved ones if allowed on an accompanied tour.

I applied for some jobs at the mall and the Government. I couldn't be in the Priority Placement Program (PPP) because my husband was in Okinawa and I was no longer on his orders. In the meantime, I took a job in the mall, selling women's lingerie, while applying for a government position at Naval Medical Center Bethesda CHRO. Sometimes it is not what you know, but who you know. I was given a women name Linda. And I called her once a week in HRO Human Resource.

One must be persistent when applying for employment, regardless of where it may be. With my positive thinking, I received a phone call for an interview for the Pediatrics and Adolescents Clinic. A few days later, I nailed that interview! With his grace, I was hired for the job. My hours were from 7:00 a.m. until 5:00 p.m. with every other Friday off. I loved it. I booked appointments and checked in kids who came to see the doctors.

I worked two jobs. I was busy, but the jobs kept me going. As usual, when I started working, my unemployment stopped. It felt I knew we would be okay. In the meantime, I was in Maryland, enjoying life and becoming stronger and more spiritual by the day.

I had lunch with a dear friend, and never in my wildest dreams knew that she was close to having a nervous breakdown. Just the idea of this news hurt me so much. She's the type of woman who held in a lot of hurt. I prayed with and for her mental health. She took medications to help with her diagnoses. I've always believed you never know someone's story. Life is something I cannot explain.

I also know some spouses who are going through some of the same things right now. We are tough, but we are human. Life is good, but we all go through different tests in our lives. You must work hard, pass life's tests, learn and grow from them, and then press on. I feel in my heart that God has always been my saving grace.

I missed my hubby so much the times I missed his call working at the mall on the weekends. I would be crushed. He could fly home for thirty days during the middle of his tour. We had a great time while he was home. We stayed up late and talked for hours. I really enjoyed my time with him, even though I knew that eventually his leave would end and he would have to go back to Okinawa, Japan. Once again, I would miss him with all my heart.

It seemed like only a week or two. Once again, the thought of being alone began to creep into my mind. When my spouse went back at the end of his leave, we talked about how hard it was being apart. We decided I would join him in Japan. After a year being apart, we felt it was the smart thing to do.

By believing in a higher power's plan and grace for me, I could face the struggles associated with being a military spouse, especially moving to a new place and getting to know a new country where I would meet other spouses and make new friends. I also absorbed lessons in staying healthy physically, mentally, and spiritually. Most important, he gave me a tough love lesson in controlling my finances, sticking to a budget, and walking away from things I couldn't have at that time. Not once did he let me down in this chapter of my life. As previously said, every time I felt I was at wit's end, he blessed me financially. Every time!

Military spouses, please remember this one thing: life's a journey! Enjoy all of it. The good and bad. The happy and the sad. Especially the tough trials in your life.

Bless you all.

Chapter 2

HARD TIMES

T he time came! Okinawa, I was on my way!

I decided to join Kyle in Okinawa because being apart was hard. I finally arrived in Japan after being in the United States without him for an entire year. A lot comes with getting ready to PCS out of country. I had to put my car in storage, which would be a cost of $200 a month. This is because the government will only pay for a family to store one vehicle while stationed outside the country. Spouses also must get shot records updated and apply for a passport. As for household goods, pack-out dates must be set so items can be shipped to you. If you live in base housing, you are required to schedule an inspection to clear base housing.

Knowing what works best for me, I sat down and made a list of everything I needed to accomplish. Each day I tackled something on that to-do list, making sure not to overwhelm myself in the process. Military spouses, always remember that when trying to complete tasks, do what you have the strength for each day. I will testify that I am never always completely together and strong. During my times of weakness, I've always prayed to my higher power to please give me patience with myself and the people I meet. Please use whatever higher power you believe in so that you don't become anxious and short with people.

When the time came for me to leave, I was both sad and happy. It was a mixed emotional situation. I knew I was going to miss my family and friends who lived in the United States. My sister Barbara knew I would miss her most- we lived ten minutes from each other. I have four sisters- Benita, Mary, Ann and Barbara. I am the youngest. Benita, Ann and Mary live in Pensacola, Florida.

I was also extremely excited to finally be with my husband again! The shuttle picked us up and took us to the airport. I cried so hard, and my mind would not stop racing. I did not want to leave my sister. We have always been so close. I was totally devastated. I wanted the best of both worlds—my family and my husband and his military career.

Kyle and Martha were headed to Okinawa, Japan.

While in San Diego, before flying to Okinawa, Kyle and I went to the House of Blues for dinner. I can honestly say that, now, I did not feel any connection to him at all. It was like getting to know him all over again since we had been apart for a little more than a year. I did not know how to reconnect with him, and this was the hardest transition for me during this period in our marriage. Some spouses may be able to reconnect easily after being away from each other so long. This was not the case for me. The time we spent apart put a big hole in our relationship. I had to learn my partner all over again, and he also had to teach me.

As we boarded our flight to Okinawa, I knew we were surely on our way to Japan. I had never flown that far before, so I felt a little on edge during the trip. It was a long flight, exactly twenty-two hours. I slept a lot during the flight. Every time I woke up, I began to feel a deep sensation of anxiety. I decided to get up and walk around. There were so many kids and military spouses on the plane. This was a flight solely for military families. Some of the kids were smiling and laughing, having fun on the trip. On the other hand, other children were upset and wouldn't stop crying. Many were tired.

A feeling of anxiety came over me, but it was of excitement due to the thought of living in a new country. I would encounter new languages and unfamiliar customs. There was also the excitement of finding and meeting new friends. I was unsure if I would be able to find a friend I could trust and get along with like my sister and friends in the United States. As we flew into Okinawa, Japan, I began to pray and thank God for bringing us safely through the flight.

We flew into and landed at Kadena Air Force Base. The island was so bright and lit with lights. This was very different for me. My hometown of Pensacola has some of the prettiest beaches in the world because of its pure, white beach sand but it is nowhere as brightly lit as the island of Japan. I immediately thought, *Goodness, I am in another country!* This life would be excited and powerful I could feel it in my bones. Joy.

After we landed, my husband and I stopped and got something to eat at a place called Hoka Hoka Ta, located right outside Kinser Marine Corps Base. It was a little shack restaurant with great chicken, rice and beef. The Japanese food was the best! I thought, *this is so funny. Just twenty-two hours ago, I was in LA, eating American food. Now, I am halfway around the world, eating authentic Japanese food. Life can't get any better than this!*

I felt the jet lag from the trip affect my body. I was extremely tired, so we turned in early on our first night in Japan. We lay in bed for a little while and then completed some much-needed pillow talk. Suddenly, I buried my head in my pillow. The tears fell hard as I began to dearly miss my sister Barbara. This was so hard and felt too much to bear. My sister Barbara and I did so many things together, like shopping. And she was my happy hour girl on Fridays. I remembered I was in Maryland for the past year. Nevertheless, I just wanted to hear my sister's voice again. Being a military spouse can be so hard. I was happy to be with my husband, but I would also love to have had my family close by.

Japan is a day ahead of the United States, so another issue I began to experience was that my sleeping pattern was off as my body and mind tried to adjust to a new time zone. I had to get my body, mind, and spirit back on track.

The next day was Sunday and I was thrilled when I bought an international long distance calling card. I immediately called my sister. I was so happy to hear her voice! We talked for quite a while, and I felt much better after our conversation.

My hubby took me sightseeing around the island and to the Post Exchange (PX) to go shopping. In my opinion, it was better shopping than any other PX I have shopped. Japan was a different world. I was on the brink of experiencing what some people call culture shock. Driving on the other side of the road, learning how to get around in town, and adjusting to a new way to live became my life.

The following Monday morning, my husband took me to the base housing on Camp Kinser, and we received the keys to our new place. The women who worked at the Housing Office Lisa, Linda, Mary, were so sweet and made me feel welcome living in Japan.

I was informed our household goods had unfortunately not yet arrived in Japan. As the saying goes, "You know the drill." So, this situation was expected from government movers and shippers. However, this time I didn't get too upset. I found it hilarious! Our household goods would arrive in Japan in a couple weeks. The days crept by slowly, but our shipment arrived, and

I was extremely happy. This time, all our items made it; nothing was missing. I began to excitedly unpack everything and put them in proper places. The house was set up, and felt like home. A home for me and Kyle. The apartment we lived in was on the third floor. High rise apartment living was new to me. This base housing was basically water front property, something I always dreamed of living.

Once again, Kyle would have deployed seven days after my coming to Japan. He deployed to Thailand for two months of our time together in Okinawa. So, he would be away again, I was now living halfway across the world from my family and friends. Especially my sister Barbara in Maryland. I tried to stay positive about the situation. It was scary. I stopped, took a deep breath and said to myself, *this is Divine Timing for you Martha. You are where you supposed to be at this time of your life put on your big girl panties.*

I applied for an Okinawa driving license. Their driving rules are totally different from the ones in the United States. For example, their traffic signs are different. There were two parts of the driving course, just as it is in Florida. The written part of the test was multiple choice. Afterward, I was required to take a driving test. I passed both tests.

It was the infancy of my living in Japan. I was still learning the island, and everywhere I looked, a lot of the language was naturally in Japanese. Yet, I was experiencing a feeling I had never felt before. I felt at peace and calm. Yes, this may be an overwhelming experience, but I was willing to learn anything and everything to better myself and enjoy this tour.

My hubby left for his deployment in Thailand. I began to think how scary it was that I could not drive ten minutes and be at my sister's house in Maryland. This type of thought entered my mind a lot during my times of boredom. Therefore, every time

I began to get bored, I prayed to get motivated and get going. I decide to learn the island of Okinawa and its language. I indulged in the amazing Japanese food at all the restaurants I passed on my learning missions. I explored the island as an archaeologist would an ancient burial site. I experienced the smell of the different foods, and visited a healing pool. I made the most of my time, learning the history and culture of Japan and its citizens. I can remember going to bed with tears about my new surroundings. But they were tears caused by the feeling of an abundance of peace and joy.

After a few weeks of adjustment, I was ready to go back to work. My first stop was the HR Civil Personnel Office on base. It only took about a month before I landed a job as a secretary on the air force base in Kadena. My typing skills were slim to none, but I knew I would go in there and do my job well. I was so happy to get the job and I took pride in my work.

It was a typical eight hours a day office job with two days off a week. I had a system set up to keep me focused and away from thoughts of how much I missed everyone. I worked my eight hours and then returned home. I changed clothes and went to the gym. I love to work out. Exercising helps with alleviating stress and depression. It also keeps you in shape, so your health is one less thing to worry about while having so many other items on your plate.

I really missed my hubby and family. When not working or at the gym, I called home to speak with family members- especially my sister. I started to realize I needed to pray on a regular basis. One should enjoy this peace on earth while we are alive. When I started to talk and walk with my higher power, he always pulled me out those feelings of misery.

It took months to adjust to the difference in times zones in Japan. This can be a very difficult adjustment and may even take months to adjust to your new time zone or way of living. However, if PCS orders allow you to travel with your military spouse, please do so. Some orders do not allow you to travel with your military spouse. Therefore, I pray that you all will be able to travel and PCS with your military spouse. What I learned caused me to grow up fast and I wish to share these blessings and experiences with everyone.

I enjoyed my job, and other military dependents in Okinawa welcomed me with open arms. They showed me the right places to visit and warned me there were some unsafe areas. I also joined their book club. The women took me out for plenty of dinners and made me feel as one of the girls. Forever glowing with a huge smile on my face, I knew all would be well with friends like these.

What I learned, being a spouse to an active duty military Marine, was that wherever the government sends you, one must make the best of every situation. You must surround yourself with go-getters, not quitters. Always surround yourself with people who lift you up and not those who tear you down.

My mom would say, "Everyone is not going to like you in life, but that is ok. Real ones will love you and embrace you as you are." I live by this mantra, and I take it to heart. I pray about everything. There have been plenty of times in my life when I made decisions without praying first, and the consequences have been tremendous. On other occasions, he has spoken to me directly about a course of action I needed to take concerning certain situations. Being the conceited person I was, I ignored my God's words and did my own thing. Those decisions I made not based on a higher power's instruction, for me always came back to bite me in my bottom. I cannot stress enough how important it is to become connected with the right people. Always use your spiritual belief, and know that your intuition is always correct. I will say there were times when I did not listen to my intuition, and boy did it get crazy. Therefore, I promised myself I would never stop listening to my spirit and intuition. They were my best friends and guided me on the right path of life and love during my overseas tour in Okinawa, Japan. I attended church on Camp Foster great service. Kadena Air Force Base has a breath-taking breakfast brunch. Love to go there after church 5 star set up. I will say over again please go overseas and enjoy the military life.

Chapter 3

....

WALKING IN MY GROWTH AND STRENGTH GROWING UP

My new life in Japan began to take its interesting course. Due to being apart during the last year, I knew my hubby and I would have to love each other all over again like we were before. Now he was away for the first two months of our tour in Okinawa, our task of rebuilding our relationship became even more daunting. It was time for me to step up and be a big girl in the game of life. Instead of sitting around, waiting for someone to show me the island, I decided to learn it on my own. God carried me as I drove all over that island.

I really became focused on working out and made sure I hit the gym every evening after work. At the gym, there were plenty of spouses who were into their bodies and keeping in shape. This made working out even more fun.

Kyle, my husband began sending me gifts and care packages from Thailand every week. There were nice silk scarfs, handbags and shoes. Excitement rushed over me every day as I went to the mailbox, anticipating the packages he sent me. I really looked forward to those packages.

Going to the gym, time flew, and his two-month deployment in Thailand was up before we knew it. A slight bit of fear began to surface as I realized the time had come for us to work on our marriage and rebuild our relationship. I prayed and asked for guidance. When he returned, we talked and started to make time for date nights. Even though I was scared to start over in this aspect of our time together, I prayed he would guide us on the right path.

My life in Okinawa was good. I could sit down and talk with plenty of other military spouses. Every spouse I spoke with had a story — some happy and some were sad. This was where I learned the lesson that spouses must remember not to lose ourselves.

However, if you have, I am here to share with you how I found myself after being lost.

At this point, my husband was back from his deployment. I began to have panic attacks, and I did not know what was going on or where they came from. The attacks were so strong I woke up at night. I was still healing from my mother's passing, which hit me hard. My hubby knew I still mourned and did not know what to do. I could see his love and care but also fear on his face when he looked at me. I made an appointment to see my doctor, and she put me on an antidepressant. I didn't like how I felt when I took that medication. My anxiety attacks would come while I was sleeping. I thought I could not breath and felt light headed when I stood. The medication made me feel as if I were walking and talking in slow motion, spacey feeling. I took the medication for two months.

Then, one night I was sleeping and had an attack that woke me. I started watching television around 3 o'clock in the morning. The program I watched was *The Midwest Center for Stress & Anxiety (Attacking Anxiety & Depression)*. I knew God would not allow me to continue this travel to the dark depths of misery. So, I was so grateful to know I was not losing my mind and I was having anxiety attacks. I ordered a copy of the workbook and cassettes. When it arrived, I began to read and complete the daily relaxation tip. I started to feel better as my panic attacks began to decrease. After a month, the attacks went from five a day to once a day. I started to relax more and eat a better diet. My thought pattern changed, and I started to pray intently about the passing of my mother. The confidence of knowing my mother would always be by my side began to comfort me and subdue my mourning.

I went back to my doctor for a follow-up appointment concerning the antidepressant medication. My doctor told me I was doing so well she completely took me off medication. She was excited to see the tapes and workbook I worked on to help me cope with life. At this moment, I knew it was the grace of God that would always guide and keep me strong.

If you are dealing with anxiety and having panic attacks, always take your prescribed medication and constantly consult your physician about any positives or negatives responses you may experience. I am only telling you what worked for me. I could better understand my body and mind. My spouse and I could have date night, and it felt good. We had no problems, and I felt no anxiety or panic attacks. Yet, I always keep in mind that I am a work in progress. His grace teaches me to never give up. We all have the strength to continue. You will win. Trust and believe me… you will win. "This I know to be truth. I can do all things through Christ which strengthens me" (Philippians 4:13 KJV).

I will never say it has been an easy road, because it has not. But I decided to take charge of my life. Anxiety and depression are hereditary in my family. Therefore, I had to learn to change my thinking, eat better, and surround myself with good, soothing things and people. This may benefit you, too, by helping to keep your life in balance. Also, find a friend you can trust. A friend you can hang out or even exercise with four day a week. I am fifty years old. Do I feel it? No, I do not. I want to live a long life? Yes, that is why I take care of me first. I only have one me, and I love her so much!

In the interest of healthy eating, I suggest you watch your intake of sweets always. As a woman, I love my curves and how they look when I am nude. This shows the confidence I have when thinking of my body and health.

Meditation twice a day is something I worked on for years. Medicine, science and history have all proved that meditation is good for the body, spirit and mind. In addition to working out and meditating, I continue to work on myself every day. To track my progress, I keep what I call a vision board where I post items about people and things I need to do. I have always taken this board to heart. So much so that I have already completed one vision board and have started a new one.

I remember this is the little girl who live in Pensacola Village. A little girl who was quiet and scared to speak up for herself. One whose sisters had to fight for over the years. As the baby girl of the family, I was a young woman with a lot of fear. I learned one day that your sisters will not always will be with you. So, I had to grow up. I am so proud of myself and the woman I became.

Please, always remember whatever you are dealing with in life, you must never give up. Never forget to give all your problems to your higher power, and be alive within yourself. Life is good, so buckle up and enjoy the ride. Being prepared will help you get through the roller-coaster ride of daily life.

There are a few books I encourage you to read:

Affirmations by Noah St. John
Pocket Prayers for Women by Joyce Myers (My favorite)

Love Yourself Heal Your Life by Louise L Hay (an amazing book)
Healing Letters by Myrtle Fillmore (one of my favorite)
Seeds of Wisdom by Mike Murdock (Love it a lot of wisdom)
The Power of Positive Thinking Norman Vincent Peal (Love this book)

I read these books all the time while forever learning and growing. Embrace life and enjoy yourself. I look forward to you all growing in your own spirit and way.

Chapter 4

FASTENING AND GROWING PAINS

I felt like I learned something good each day of every month. I began to explore more and more with the Okinawan natives. I learned a lot from those Japanese women, and they learned quite a bit from me. I learned about their basic foods, rice seaweed sushi and great stores to shop. So, I want all of you spouses who are at home to get out more in Okinawa, Japan. There are so many programs and activities to do with your family. I enjoyed the fashion shows on base, Kadena free movie nights, spouse's night out, and children's play groups. There are so many programs designed to keep your family busy. Neither you nor your children should ever experience boredom. You just must do your research to find out what works best for you and your family.

Starting a journal is a strong recommendation. I started writing in my personal journal at the age 25. I had a lot to say — about my feelings, my body, people I chose to have in my life and great people who just showed up in my life. I was not happy with my body or how I was eating unhealthy, fatty foods and sweets. I put my body in a workout mode, started to put more green vegetables in my body and drank eight glasses of water a day. Putting my thoughts on paper helped to ease the mind and I started to see good progress in my body, mind, soul and spirit. Writing in a journal also helped me make it through the months my husband was away. It helped me feel better, and my mind cleared. I made sure to put myself in a positive circle and around strong people. "Your life is what you make of it," that is the truth. You must find a task that works for you. My growing pains were when I trusted so-called girlfriends and spilled out my heart to them, only to find out they told other people my business. I was there topical in the conversations and it broke my spirit. I was shocked and hurt, I will not speak on what was talked about I will say know the people you call friends. To me this was growing pains and becoming stronger and smarter about the definitions of FRIENDS.

When I stayed focused and kept my faith, everything fell properly into place. I just smiled and kept my head up. I learned my heart is big. I enjoy helping people by giving words of encouragement and letting them know they are not alone. But you must want the help yourself first before you can help anyone else. That is why I decided to come in to my womanhood at the age of 25 in Pensacola Village. I feel in my heart I have saved so many spouses. It let me know I'm on the right page when a spouse says "Thank you. I was going to walk away from my marriage. Talking with you let me know I am not alone, Mrs. Martha."

Everything I have gained and learned as a spouse made me stronger and smarter. I am happy to say I was blessed to travel and see the world, meeting some wonderful families. When I think of how far I have come, my heart is filled with joy. Yet, I always say you must grow up fast as a military spouse, and I am still growing.

I smiled with excitement as I worked and saved, watching our bank account grow. You can really save a nice little nest egg and become debt-free while stationed overseas in Okinawa Japan. When you return to the United States, you can pay off all your bills, buy your dream car for a good price, travel to different countries, and enjoy yourself. Remember, there will come a time your spouse will put up his or her hat, so take advantage of this blessing while you can. Please enjoy traveling the world.

We saved and paid off all our bills. One thing I learned was how to budget money and hold the house down. My mother and grandparents taught me a lot concerning family finances. My grandparents were entrepreneurs when I was just a young girl. My grandparents were hard workers. Consequently, they preached hard work. Nothing comes easily in life. And if it did, there were actions and consequences behind it. Basically, there would be nothing good about it. If you have not received your blessings in life yet, it is time to receive them right now. Even if something is only $1, $5, $10, $20, or $25, it's something, it is a start. Seeing a positive result from anything will make you work harder. I know things get better. I have been there before, and I am so proud of how far we have come. Anything is possible. Believe me. I am proof of a work in progress.

I enjoyed Okinawa so much, even during those trying times in my marriage. Being married to any active duty member is hard. Their working hours are sometimes long, and the higher the rank, the larger the responsibilities. I feel everyone flows in their own ways. In all, make sure to always take care of you, and make the best decisions. I learned that family and close friends can give their advice, but you must really make your own smart choices in life.

Some people call this karma. Unfortunately, karma can be good or bad. To me, this means what we experience in life is based on the many decisions we make throughout our lives. If we make good, sound, spiritually based decisions, life will be okay. However, if one makes nothing but bad and negative decisions, he or she will tend to live a life of turmoil and toxicity. And you could {make good decisions. Life is a journey—good and bad things come in our lives.} Having the right tools will get you through growing pains. Now I must speak on fasting- this is a tool I started to do in 2006 praying and seeking answer from my God sometimes I felt like my back was up against the wall, the only thing I was taught is to pray. Fastening for me I started off four hours a day, know all day when that comes into my heart to do.

Be happy and healthy on your journey!

Chapter 5

DECISIONS ARE POWERFUL

I t's May 2005, and we are back in the United States from our tour in Japan. How great it feels to be back in the United States! Our new PCS orders are to Inspector and Instructor (I & I) Duty in Memphis, Tennessee. On this tour, my spouse trained the Marine Reserve. I made it back to the continental United States just in time for my niece's and nephew's graduations from high school. Man, time does fly by so fast. I feel relieved I am still a spouse.

So, back to the drawing board looking for employment. Those on the outside looking in may think military life is great. It's a good life, but many don't realize how burned out setting up your new home, getting the kids in school, and learning the area can make you. There is quite a bit of moving plus a lot of hustle and bustle. I remember days when I sat around with other military wives who were new to the game and did not know anything. I made sure to pass much information and support to them that I could. Like how to prepare yourself for your next duty station by reading up on the place. This includes finding out in advance, what areas are good to live in, if there are no base housing, learning about schools, and the job market.

Staying prayed up is why I am still standing. During my years of traveling all over the world, I always made the best out of it.

Martha E. H. Franklin

Then, my oldest sister, Benita, was diagnosed with amyotrophic lateral sclerosis (ALS). We had only been back in the United States for about six months. It took a lot out of the family. I was happy to be back in the States so I could go home as much as I could. However, life situations still hurt. Benita was the angel of the family. She passed away.

ALS is a degenerative neurological disease that attacks the nerve cells. People with ALS eventually die when they are no longer able to breathe on their own. According to the National Institutes of Health, in 90 percent to 95 percent of cases, the disease strikes without the individual having any known risk factors. A hereditary component is found in approximately 5 percent of cases. We watched our loved ones pass away, and there was nothing anyone could do. I prayed so much for strength and guidance, not only for me but for my family as well. For Benita's kids and her husband, I am full of tears right now thinking about her.

Once again, I was back on the PPP list for another GS position with the federal government in Millington, Tennessee. I interviewed for the three years I was there and never got a government job. I finally got a job after applying for placements in town. It was the first time this happened to me while using the PPP program. Now I had to work in town, at Talbots. I was totally shocked.

We make it happen as a military spouse. The military does it part for the family, but I feel spouses of active duty military members and Department of Defense (DOD) civilians could use a little more support. This is when I step in with my faith and bring out my skills. I stop overthinking things then I pray about it and let it go. Maybe one's job can be transferred, so you will have a position when you arrive at your new post. My higher power does not want people to be stressed, so I turned my thinking around and started to work hard at Talbots- a job I really enjoyed. And I did well!

My goal is to touch as many spouses as I can with this book. God has changed my pattern of life, and I wish to share my blessed technique with all of you. I have a plan of working hard and traveling around the world to touch spouses everywhere. I want to be able to talk about people's mindfulness and spirits and how they operate in our daily lives. Here's a small plan for you to start with. Just please remember to always do what works best for you.

- Start your morning with quotes. Norman Vincent Peale *The Power of Positive Thinking*. I recommend this book to everyone.
- Then take some quiet time to pray and meditate, or just sit still for a few minutes. Do what works for you, but take time out of your day just for you. If you cannot do this in the morning, put the kids down for nap, and let your mind relax and take deep breaths. I always put my mind on a beach in Hawaii, listening to the water.
- Picture yourself somewhere on that favorite island. If you're a young spouse and have never been away from family, this could be a shock to you. For all my young spouses with kids or are expecting their first child, I am praying for you. I hope you are reading the book, and I can help you in many ways. I know you are scared. Maybe you are even thinking, *what have I gotten myself into?*
- Always remember that you must make time for yourself. Surround yourself in positives settings.
- Make sure to get out of the house. There are seven days in a week; get out at least six of them.

- Find a chapel on base or a church home, regardless whatever faith you believe in. Search out free actives to engage in and find positives circles of people to be around.

I lived for my husband for a long time and did not have a life for myself. I experienced horrible panic attacks. They put me on medication which made me feel spacey and out of touch. I awoke one morning and started to pray for this to leave my body and mind. I started to meditate and changed my way of thinking and my social company. I realized fear took over my life, so I started to live my life one day at a time. I loved my husband, but I must take care of myself first. I will always love me unconditionally.

Give yourself a big hug in the morning to start your day. You must find a way to release yourself and the tension in your life. I started to be my own women and live for Martha. I love the snapshot of my life today.

Fear can rule your life if you allow it. I learned I am not shy. I was told when I was a child by family, I am a long way from being shy so I grew up thinking I was. Never spoke up for myself. The last thing you would catch me doing as a little girl was speaking out to the world. We live in a world where you must speak up and have a voice. Each person contains strength and a voice for the world to hear. We just need to pull it out of our bodies at the right time. Being in Okinawa was a big difference from living in the United States. I have grown so strong from being away from family and taking care of myself. I chose to get out there and explore my surroundings, although my heart pounded and my mind raced with fear. I got through it. When you start to feel, stress coming upon you, distract yourself. Walk away from it. Find peace within yourself. Just take things one day at a time.

During hard times, it seems like everything in the world crashes on top of me. My sister was not doing well, so I went to Florida to visit her. I stayed at the hospital all night. Being in someone's presence means so much to me. I was so blessed to be able and sit in her presence.

In 2006, I started tithing 10 percent of my earnings. And boy, did my life change for the better! Yes, it did. This is what worked for me, but I am not telling anyone to jump on board with this decision. I am only telling you what works best for me. Giving 10 percent was not a lot of money for me. On top of that, I was engaged in a life workout pattern by going to the gym, walking, and meditating. Or even reading a book under a tree. I also love listening to relaxation music and staying focused on my life goals. Always make sure you are eating good, healthy foods to help improve your body, mind and soul. I have come a long way during my travels in life.

Good luck on your journey, and be blessed.

Chapter 6

THE WAY IT IS

I am sitting here thinking about this book, my life, and sharing my story with other military spouses, and civilians all over the world. My life, by far, has not been peaches and cream. We were next stationed in Jacksonville, North Carolina. There was not a lot to do or see here. It was nowhere close to being as an exciting place as Okinawa, Japan. But you suck it up, and make the best of it. The next, large city was forty-five minutes away, and I worked on the second-largest Marine Corps base in the world.

I had grown up and become a powerful and strong woman. It was time to live my purpose, which is to become an author and to have my organization, Women of Fruit and Label, which will prepare a snapshot of your life to help guide you in the right direction. It was time for me to branch out and do my own thing. You must live out your own dreams. Do not try and live through your military or civilian spouse's life. I had no social life of my own. This was one of the biggest mistakes I made. But I turned things around. I became more engaged in reading about small business and going to workshops.

We are in a new year; girlfriends, family, and coworkers are still the same. You have to make a decision in your life to answer the question, "What is healthy for me?" This decision must come from the heart. I've realized in life that in order to grow, I really had to let things and people go. Never forget the people in your life, but limit your space and circle. I know it is hard, but I'm a firm believer that there is a season for everything. It can hurt and even get lonely at times. From experience, I learned this is the best way to handle the situations. Missing girl-time trips is one thing I really hate, yet I also see how my life has change for the better. Now I make smarter and wiser decisions, which caused me to accomplish a lot.

My life must be spiritually strong at all times. If you are not doing what you enjoy, you will not put your all into it. I have come to understand myself. I have learned who I am and what I want in life to live in a healthy, spiritual way. I have learned everyone cannot go where you are going in life. God has a plan for you and the people he has chosen for your life. I would never tell anyone to walk away from their friends, family, marriage or coworkers. Be careful of the circle you are in or around.

I have grown up so much during my life as a military spouse. I still feel Marines are good men and women. They work hard, but some do not know how to balance home and duty. Most of the time, spouses and children go through hard times. There are Marines who know how to balance it all.

My hubby has always been dedicated to his job. For a long time, he was not dedicated to me or the household. I felt we could get things right if he was willing to work on them. It takes two to pull through a marriage. I noticed early in our marriage we are different creatures. I tried to change him but ended up draining myself. So, for me, I am feeding my soul and have let go of trying to change others.

I love life, and most of all, I love me. Working with Marines can be a highly stressful job. The cases I see cause me to pray constantly for all of our members of the armed forces. Since I've come in contact with many different things in my life as a military spouse, I pray my book touches a lot of lives in many ways. It has definitely been a ride. Life has its ups and downs. As we get knocked down, we must vigilantly remember to get back up and keep on trying until you get it right. I believe everyone has a gift and a story to share. I also know in the core of my bones that I have graduated from so many of life's lessons. Mind you, that's a graduation with all straight A's! As for my husband, I will always love him but not live through him. This is a great time in my life, even in sad times. It's time to take off your boots, hang your handbags, and relax.

Chapter 7

TAKING OFF YOUR BOOTS AND HANGING UP YOUR HANDBAG

Most military spouses usually put in forty hours or more a week at work. On the other hand, I cannot count how many hours our active duty military members put in a week. I remember how my husband worked from sunup to sundown. As civilians, we come home for the evening and keep on our work clothes, or we need to change into something comfortable. We clean up around the house and cook dinner. Let's not forget about helping the kids with homework and getting them settled for the night. When an active duty military member enters the door, he or she is still in uniform while talking about the crazy day at the unit. The spouse listens while still trying to complete eight more tasks at the same time. All the while, everyone is talking a mile a minute, and no one is breathing or coming up for air. To eliminate this issue in your family, you have to first remember to keep discussion about your day at work, short and sweet. Do not dwell on that day. I spent some crazy days at work- the more I talked about it, the more it drained me. Again, I am only speaking for myself.

Once you enter the door, take off your work clothes and get into something comfortable. Put something relaxing on to calm your mind from the day. From here, you can start your duties in the home such as homework with the kids, or starting dinner for the family. Make sure to spend some time with your kids. It is so important to their social development. I do know you and your spouse have to make some time together as well. Maybe after putting the kids to bed you can chill with each other, even if it's only talking for twenty minutes. You need that bond.

Greet your spouse when he or she walks in the door. Your spouse might be a little more comfortable if he or she were to change out of work clothes as soon as they get home. By the time your military spouse has returned, he or she will also feel more relaxed and ready to unwind from the day. Maybe you two can talk about what's for dinner or how the children are doing in school. If you really need to speak about your workday with your spouse, limit the conversation to the minimum, and focus on enjoying your time with your family.

I have learned your home is your place of refuge from the rest of the world. I always love walking into my home, knowing I am getting ready to chill and relax. You have to turn your home into your treasure. Find a room in the house where you can relax and that makes you smile. Put something personal in that area —a pillow, book, blanket, a cup for your warm tea, or an iPod with your favorite music. Trust me, it works.

I talk about hanging up your handbag. Handbags are weighed down with so many things. It may include unhealthy things from the work environment, such as items I had to accomplish before the end of the week. I had to learn to hang up the bag and take life one day at a time. Do not let negative things creep into your mind. Take care of yourself. We all are put on this earth to enjoy life. Therefore, I say hang up your handbag when you enter the door; military members, remember to take off your boots.

Enjoy your afternoon, and relax the day away. Find time for each other. This is what we all call family time. Always make a great effort to have dinner together. With this in mind, try your best to always eat dinner at the dinner table. Studies have shown that children do better in life and school when they are taught to eat at the dinner table. This is also when spouses can talk to and be open ears for each other. Make time for each other and your family. Always love each other. Always! Regardless of the good or bad times.

Chapter 8

BUILDING YOUR FAITH

I can do all things through Christ which strengthens me.

Philippians 4:13 (KJV)

I t was Christmastime 2007. We were enjoying our new home in Jacksonville and Kyle was at war. I chose not to buy a tree. I am happy and relaxed with no gifts. Thoughts of service members in war, fighting and losing their lives, went through my mind. That means way more to me than shopping. This is when I knew my life was back on the right track.

I'm so happy and humbled to know how to love myself. Especially coming from stressed-out life battles with my parents. I've realized how to take myself to the next level and live even in my darkest times. Sometimes I just get so full from joy, and I love it! I would not trade it for anything in the world. I have shared this with you to let someone know they are not alone.

I have been an employee for the government. I worked with active duty members. My team and I formed the Post-(PDHRA). I enjoyed my fellow coworkers and leadership. I am not perfect by any means. Actually, I am a long way from it. In all my years, together 15 years working for Government, I truly enjoyed my time before I stepped away- for good.

I was driving home one day and realized the job was not for me anymore. I had to move on with my dreams of becoming an author because life is too short. I dreamt big about being on the New York Times Best Seller List. Therefore, I walked away with about $2,000.00 in my account and a lot of faith. However, I chose to change my lifestyles by staying healthy and living a spiritually strong way of life. Nonetheless, I knew I was working in an unhealthy environment. I would usually say, "stick it out until you have something else in line." This time, I walked out in faith. I had to write this non-fiction book about my life as a spouse to save as many people I could. So, I left my last government job May 27, 2011.

Divorce rates are on the rise. Statistics say 3.7 percent military marriages ended in 2011. I wonder if that will ever change. Honestly, I do not know. Getting counseling and learning how to balance your marriage and your life are good ways to start trying to save our marriages. It can be hard to get your spouse to go to counseling. I have learned that it is a two-way street; both people have to work together in this matter. You cannot save your family by yourself.

My hubby and I were on another tour. He deployed to Afghanistan. It was so hard for him to be away again. I continued to work out at the gym, and made a valiant effort to put myself in positive circles and around positive people. We as spouses are in a fight as well, just not in the war. I pray every day for our troops all over the world and their families. Until you stand in a spouse's shoes, you cannot fully relate to our lives. I missed the good times with my husband. The little things, like his boots sitting by the door, or always talking to him. I looked around the house, and it was so quiet. What kept me going was my faith. I knew he would return to me. It's even harder for spouses with children because if the children are small, they do not understand what's going on. What worked for me has been just staying focused. I worked on my manuscript and read a lot of books. If you have kids, find a playgroup for them while hanging out with other parents so that you can interact with them as well as feed the body and soul with good things and good people.

I know I worked hard, and I can do anything if I put my mind to it. Becoming a military spouse made me work hard in a lot of ways. I was on the committee for Toys for Tots in Memphis and enjoyed it. Key Volunteer is another program that I hear is awesome. These opportunities are available for any spouses who would love to get involved. I talk about our Marines a lot in this book. No one is perfect. Work out whatever you can with your spouses. They are good men and women.

My husband's tour ended after thirty-two weeks, roughly two hundred and twenty days. Yet, the mission did not stop there. He was home for four weeks and then packed up to attend school in Quantico, Virginia. I could have taken this news poorly and made myself sick and upset, But I chose to do none of that because he was still going, and there was nothing I could do about it. I took it in peacefully, stayed focused, and worked on my goals. Yes, he had just returned from war and was going away again. At the end of the day, he was doing what he enjoyed. He worked hard with other service members to defend this great nation. I will not let myself fall into that sad shell again. That is why I cannot stop saying, "Find the things you love to do to keep your mind on track." I want all my spouses out there to work hard on yourself and stay focused. Whatever religious or spiritual beliefs you may have, believe in them and use them. I want you all to take care of yourself and feel good.

This is a very sensitive subject. Believe it when I tell you that I was once heavy-hearted. When my mom turned ill, I did nothing but eat all the time as a result of feeling sad and lonely. I was so upset that I did not have my mom around. My sister talked with me about my weight and the quick gain she witnessed. I was upset with her acknowledgment, but at the same time, I knew she loved me and wanted me to be in good health. We started a menu plan. Boy, did we change! I lost a bulk of the weight by walking. I started off slowly by power walking and then eventually moved up to running. I dropped three dress sizes. Now, you cannot keep me out of the gym. I just love it! And to think-- I was the girl who *hated* working out! I began eating a lot of vegetables and fruits. But I didn't eat too many of them because of their sugar content. I went cold turkey—I stopped eating bread and I consumed a lot of water.

I am not a nutritionist, but I can say this system is what worked for me. It is always recommended to get a physical exam before you start working out to make sure your body is healthy enough to begin. Your physician is also a great place to begin seeking advice on a workout regime. Never think you cannot overcome life's obstacles because you can. Just please get the faith you need, and believe in yourself.

Looking in the mirror daily, I always notice how much I love me. How much I love my curves. Basically, I love everything about me. In addition, I trust me! I know that every day is a work in progress for Mrs. Franklin.

The year 2010 was a good one. I was at Camp Lejeune, working on post, and a military spouse. I did a lot of things. The number one thing I enjoyed — and still enjoy — is writing. It is like I am on cloud nine when I am doing the things I enjoy. It is always beneficial to get other people's opinions about life's situations. Consequently, I sat down with some military spouses. I interviewed them for this book and heard how they felt about the war. The interview is discussed in the following chapter.

This the day the Lord has made; we will rejoice and be glad in it. (Psalm 118:24 KJV)

Chapter 9

NOT SEEING BUT BELIEVING

I want you to think about the things you pray for and are not receiving in your life. Please keep your faith because it is working for you. I remember a time I would get ready to move to another duty station and work myself up months before we would PCS. I worried about another job, new surroundings, and the people I would have to get to know all over again. Not to mention having to learn a new city or country and then leave that area just a year or two later. I prayed and let it go. I also had to put faith in my mind. I always knew it would turn out well. Faith always works, so I always pray.

My words of encouragement have opened a lot of doors for military spouses and many civilians around the world. The ranks have become a sensitive subject. Consequently, one of the most important things I learned from being a military spouse is that you do not have to be part of a clique. Just being you will take you a long way. I have run into so many spouses that were not very peaceful to be around them. On the other hand, I have come in contact with others, married to senior ranking members, that are humble. Yet, I've also met those who do nothing but sleep, eat, and breathe their loved ones' ranks. In those situations, it is hard to tell who the active duty member is and who is not. Those types of military spouses I find to be quite different. They usually have their own little cliques. I feel in my heart there are spouses out there who are looking to complete themselves in great ways.

I was a military spouse, and my husband was in the war. I prayed for his safety every day. Military spouses do not know what they are seeing, and that can be scary. Therefore, I am working hard to talk with spouses and teach them how to take care of themselves. I learned your life is what you make of it. I've chosen to have my own life and to work hard on my personal goals. I had to do what is healthy for me. I was so tired of anxiety and living a lie.

With that in mind, I say to everyone, "Please take care of you." Try to use me as an example because I took my faith to the highest level I possibly could. I talked to my higher power and worked on myself. In the end, I got the results I sought. In other words, it's not seeing but believing. It's faith.

Whatever high power you believe in, always seek it. Find your own purpose in life and work hard on it. I've always found author Norman Vincent Peale has some great quotations that will definitely get you motivated for your day. I continue to read and relax with my cue cards every day. I firmly believe in using them often.

Never forget to dream big! For this alone, I am a prime example. No one would ever believe that Martha would write a book. While it scared me when I first thought about it, once I started, I became more driven to write this guide for my fellow military spouses and civilians.

Unfortunately, I do not have any children of my own. I've always wanted to adopt a child, and one day I will. Nevertheless, I will continue to keep moving forward with my goals. Never will I stop dreaming, and never will I stop accomplishing my dreams. Get on board with me, and enjoy the ride of your life! You see, life is what you make of it. And it definitely helps when you have a good and positive support system. I could remember people saying crazy, negative things to me like, "Girl, you are going to write a book? I hope it works for you... Not a good idea." When you see a dream killer, immediately turn your head and go the other way. The one thing in life you don't need is to be involved with this type of people. Once again, always remember to put yourself in positive circles and around positive people.

....

Chapter 10

THE WAR

War is destructive. I don't understand why we always seem to be fighting. My husband was a first sergeant in the Marine Corps, and he was in the midst of it. He always participated in many activities with duty members and their families. I experienced nights when it was hard to sleep, so on those nights, I prayed feverishly. I thanked God for not letting it stress me out. I am human, and I worried even when I said I wouldn't. I'd constantly think about my spouse and his unit and their safety abroad. I also always thought about staying strong and positive for myself. I needed to be strong for him, because I had no idea what he and other Marines saw and dealt with while in combat. Military spouses carry a lot on our shoulders.

When life feels too heavy, I pray and give it to God.

You see, we all have different feelings about the war. Families and children do not understand war as well as military personnel. I want war to end, but I understand there will always be a mission for Marines. I pray every night God will be in control in whatever I must face. Sometimes I feel drained and extremely tired. Those are the days I just want to throw in the towel, but I choose to keep going.

I dream big, and I reach goals to achieve my dreams each day of my life. When you feel the pressure, and feel like throwing in the towel, think about how each of us has been given a gift given by a higher power. We are put on this earth to receive nothing but good. It took me a couple years to realize how I was growing and understanding my place on this small planet.

I sat down with a prior active duty member, Linda. When I interviewed her, she had a lot to say. I had the pleasure of completing my interview inside her amazing home. Linda talked about when she discovered she was pregnant. Linda was on active duty, getting ready to deploy in the Iraq War. Once she found out hers was a high-risk pregnancy, her doctors denied her deployment with her unit. Linda's husband was there for the delivery, but left when the baby was only eight months old. However, the baby was able to say her first words before her father left. And those first words were "Da Da."

After her husband left, Linda had her Marine Corps family. Her immediate family was miles away on the East Coast. She leaned on her brother-in-law for a short time since he was also an active duty Marine. Linda explained to me that life was very scary and lonely for her.

Her doctor put her on light duty, but she could work. She took the baby to work with her until day care opened. Linda's day consisted of picking up the baby in the afternoon and going back to work until she completed her day. As military spouses, we juggle to get through the moment. She never stopped taking care of the baby and her job. I know active duty and DOD civilian spouses miss many first steps and first words.

I do not have anything against going home when husbands deploy. On the other hand, I would suggest staying back, if you can. I grew up fast and was more independent when my husband was stationed away from me. Even though you may feel lonely, get out and get to know new people in your area. Make sure to learn about the town. Our military protects the world each day, so we can sleep in peace each night. There will be plenty of days and nights when you will be alone. Have faith your soldier will return to you.

I experienced my share of ups and downs as a Marine spouse. My husband served twenty-three years before hanging up his hat and taking off his boots permanently. It was a roller coaster between us, but we both stepped up to the plate and worked it out. Keeping our marriage together will always be a mission in our lives. We are preparing for his life as a civilian, so who knows what will happen. One thing I do know is that he has lived life as a Marine in tents stretched across this country and the world's deserts. This new path in his life will be a big adjustment for him.

His unit lost a service member in October 2010, during their time in the war. My spouse will never forget that day nor that service member. So I have to help him in any way I can.

If your spouse leaves the military, give him tips on applying for government positions. Explain to your spouse that the civilian world is not as structured as the one he or she has served. There could be a lot of drama as a result of the changes.

I also had the pleasure to interview HM3 Aaron Lewis. When we talked, he explained to me that he was in the war back in 2007. All Aaron talked about was sand and sandboxes. He had to put his rucksack around the door, so the sand would not blow into his tent. Descriptions of how dangerous and harsh sandstorms were filled his conversation with me. Lewis talked about how the sky would turn the deepest of orange. He said he would go back if he was in Iraq, but he is getting ready to retire. The war to him is what the military should be over there. We both agreed that there are some things and experiences he will never forget from his time in the Middle East. Lewis decided that some topics and discussions were too painful to relive, so we did not discuss those instances. My heart goes out to Lewis and all troops and DOD civilians around the world, defending our great country.

I would say again, bless all our military.

I also had the pleasure of interviewing my husband. He said he had no feelings, he just took care of his Marines and sailors. He feels the war will last about five more years. I asked my husband what feelings he had when he was deployed to the Middle East. He said he had no feelings; he just took care of his Marines. He stayed focused and on the top of the job at hand. There were good days for the units, and there were bad ones.

When the Marines returned to the United States, William felt he was responsible for his unit and made sure to take care of them. He also made sure that he helped and sought programs for his soldiers in need.

I feel everyone who has ever been to war has a story. I talked about families and marriages while my husband spoke about being a Marine and giving 110 percent in everything you do. When he or she returns home, the service member will realize the family and marriage may be falling apart. You may also realize you need to be there for your spouse.

I asked him if he would go back. He explained to me that if he had to, he would go back to war. He understands that he is older now, and his body does not work like it did when he was younger. He has served his twenty-three years and has enjoyed every bit of it! I feel being a Marine will always be in his blood. He will just have to find a new way of being comfortable in his own skin. He is getting better each day. But I know as a spouse he will never forget those experiences. With him walking as a civilian now, life is somewhat a different world for him. He is having to learn a new way of dealing with people and a new type of work environment.

He is a great man and represented the Marine Corps very well. He is the love of my life! I am so proud of him.

Thank you to everyone I had the pleasure of interviewing for this guide for military and DOD civilian spouses

Chapter 11

THE FRUIT OF THE SPIRIT

There was a dark time of my life. The walls closed in on me. In October 2012, I noticed everything turned against me. I could not understand why. The month before, I asked God to use me as his vessel and let me walk in my truth. And the result surprised me. Because I had been born again, I never knew darkness would attack me like it did. What I learned is when you decide to live right, the darkness can still come against you.

Things started to happen. So-called friends' dark energy started to come against me. Phone conversations were short and dry. For a while, I lost contact with family members. Basically, things were stripped from me and all I could do was cry and pray.

At one point, I cried, "why is this happening to me, God?" The next morning, I awoke to God speaking to me. He said, "You are on a spiritual journey in your life, and people will be dismissed from you." I cried so much my head hurt. My eyes were so puffy. I remember the Spirit spoke to me, "Where I am carrying you is a process. It will get even harder."

The long suffering was part of my journey. I watched my life transform, and I walk a different path now. At the time, I was lost. What I remember the most is how I was seeking and stood tall against the dark time. Fear was so big. I know in my heart and mind I am covered by my God and my angels. So, every morning,

I got up, put on the Armor of God, fought and stood tall in my battle. There is a person reading this book who is dealing with something working against their family or marriage. Stand tall in the battle and do not give up. Trust the Higher Power. Cover yourself in prayer. Meditate on peace; sit still and focus on all above. Teach yourself how to let go, and let the power you believe in guide you.

My life has changed so much, and I now have a clear mind. My dreams are coming to life. There is healing in my life, and I am released of things that do not serve any good. I really walk in great and healthy energy. I stopped picking my circle now I allow my God to bring in my life who he wants me to embrace. The fruit of the Spirit is real. Live, trust, and have faith. See what happens. It will take your breath away. I am living proof. I can speak on this experience because I lived in it. The fruit of the Spirit is alive and working in my life every day. Remember you must go through hard times and difficulties to receive the good in life.

These days, I am fabulous! I'm living life and enjoying my journey. I will always be a Marine spouse and I am so proud of that. Peace to you all. The fruit of the Spirit is traveling to the light. Now it is so bright it takes your breath away. Enjoy!

WORKBOOK

Exploring Your Thoughts on Paper

1. What are some things that still haunt your day and night?

2. What are some things that have stopped you from growing?

3. Does fear rule your life? If yes, please explain. If no, please explain.

4. Do you put yourself first? If not, please explain?

5. Do you feel that you live through your spouse's and /or children's lives?

6. What are you going to do to live for yourself?

7. What are you going to do to start a new day and a new life?

8. Are you still holding hurt and anger in your heart?

9. What are you going to do to let it go?

10. Can you forgive right now? Let go of what is hurting and holding you back and write it down.

11. Have you ever felt that you have made an unhealthy decision in life?

12. How would you get past those unhealthy decisions?

Do You Love Yourself?

1. How often do you pamper yourself?

2. How often do give yourself a hug?

3. Are you willing to take that extra mile for yourself?

4. Do you have ladies' or guy's night out?

5. How often do you sit still?

6. Do you ever step outside your box?

7. Have you ever had a vacation? If so, when was the last one?

8. What is the next chapter in your life?

9. Do you feel you like a safe person? If not, please explain.

10. What is making you feel unsafe? Is it fear If so explained.

11. What things are you going to work on to better yourself? Please explain.

12. How often do you allow that wall to come down and feel that soft, gentle side of you?

13. How often do you find time to relax?

14. What do you feel completes you in life?

Positives Circle

1. Do you associate with a healthy circle of people?

2. How are you going to act on matters in your life?

3. Do you have a journal? If not, please buy one.

4. Will you start writing your feelings down, gradually replacing them with something positive thoughts?

5. What are you going to do to be true to yourself? Please explain.

6. Do you feel comfortable in your own skin? Please explain.

7. How often do you curl up in a chair or bed and read a good, positive, spiritual book with a cup green tea or hot chocolate?

8. Positive thinking is powerful. What can you do to empower your thoughts and affirmations?

9. How will you being to start each and every day from this point forward Please explain.

I would love to receive feedback, on any chapter
or questions from the workbook.

Please feel free to contact me at: womenoffruitandlabel@gmail.
com Please remember I am a military spouse and a former DOD
employee who has walked in your shoes in some shape or form
or fashion.

Love you all!

God Bless

Positives Power

I can do all things in Christ who strengthens me. (Philippians 4:13 KJV)

Happiness is something that comes into our lives through doors we don't even remember opening. (Rose Wider Lane)

Printed in the United States
By Bookmasters